Literary Newsmakers for Students, Volume 1

Project Editor: Anne Marie Hacht

Editorial: Sara Constantakis and Ira Mark Milne **Rights Acquisition and Management**: Margaret Chamberlain-Gaston and Sue Rudolph **Manufacturing**: Drew Kalasky

Imaging: Lezlie Light, Mike Logusz, and Kelly Quin **Product Design**: Pamela A. E. Galbreath **Vendor Administration**: Civie Green

Product Manager: Meggin Condino

For more information, contact
Gale, an imprint of Cengage Learning
27500 Drake Rd.
Farmington Hills, MI 48331-3535
Or you can visit our internet site at

agency, institution, publication, service, or individual does not imply endorsement of the editors or publisher. Errors brought to the attention of the publisher and verified to the satisfaction of the publisher will be corrected in future editions.

ISBN 1414402813
ISSN 1559-9639

Printed in the United States of America
10 9 8 7 6 5 4 3 2 1

The Lovely Bones

Alice Sebold 2002

Introduction

In her first novel, *The Lovely Bones* (2002), Alice Sebold delves into the horror and trauma resulting from by the rape and murder of a young girl. The novel arose from Sebold's own experience with violence—her rape as an eighteen-year-old college freshman. Similar to her 1999 memoir, *Lucky*, which details her own rape, its psychological aftermath, and the arrest, trial, and conviction of the rapist, *The Lovely Bones* refuses to sanitize sexual violence. Yet the novel does not sensationalize violence either; instead, it offers the ordinariness of it. Both the setting in suburban Philadelphia, and the time period of the early 1970s, underscore Sebold's belief that no one is immune from violence; it touches everyone. More importantly, the story of Susie Salmon and her family exposes the way in which society marginalizes the victims of violence. *The Lovely Bones* becomes a study of the effects of violence, in this case rape and murder, not only on the victim, but on her family, friends, and community.

The Lovely Bones does not focus on evil; it does not attempt to make sense of bad people or bad acts. Instead the novel investigates issues of loss and grief, life and death, identity and self, remembrance and forgetting, womanhood and motherhood, coming of age and rites of passage, and heaven and earth. The readers watch with Susie as her father, mother, sister, brother, and grandmother, as well as her middle school friends, her killer, and the lead detective on the case, confront similar issues in their attempts to understand their grief. While the novel raises many questions, it does not, in fact, answer all of them. Sebold examines traditional views, such as those about heaven, sexuality, and the place of women in American society, while simultaneously challenging those views.

Author Biography

Alice Sebold was born in 1963 and grew up in the suburbs surrounding Philadelphia. In her essay "The Oddity of Suburbia," she confesses that she despised suburbia, but after living in both Manhattan and Southern California, she "realiz[ed] … that within the suburban world of [her] upbringing there were as many strange stories as there were in the more romanticized parts of the world." Her novel, *The Lovely Bones* (2002), reflects her realization that suburbia can and does contain "a bottomless well of narrative ideas." However, that realization did not occur until Sebold left Philadelphia.

In 1981, as an eighteen-year-old freshman at Syracuse University in New York, Sebold was severely beaten and raped. Rather than remain quiet about the incident, she was instrumental in the arrest, trial, and conviction of her assailant. While at Syracuse University, Sebold took writing classes with poet Tess Gallagher and fiction writer Tobias Wolff, both of whom encouraged her to remember and write about her rape. Sebold graduated from Syracuse in 1984 and entered, but did not complete, a master of fine arts degree program at the University of Houston. Instead, she moved to New York City, and as she details in the epilogue to her 1999 memoir, *Lucky*, she turned to alcohol and heroin as she struggled to come to terms with her rape. During these years, Sebold taught writing classes at Hunter College and Bucknell College in New York, worked odd jobs, and wrote. She left New York for California in 1995 and entered the M.F.A. program at the University of California, Irvine, earning her degree in 1998.

Sebold began *The Lovely Bones* during her graduate writing studies, but recognized that until she confronted and narrated her own story, she could not write the story of Susie, the main character and narrator of *The Lovely Bones*. As many critics rightly note, the two books, *Lucky* and *The Lovely Bones*, seem to be companion pieces. *The Lovely Bones* garnered two major awards, the Bram Stoker Award for best first novel and the American Booksellers Association's "Book of the Year Award." While at UC Irvine, Sebold met Glen David Gold, a fellow master's student. They married in 2001, the same year his novel *Carter Beats the Devil* was published. As of 2005, Sebold and Gold lived in California.

Plot Summary

Chapters 1-2

Fourteen-year-old Susie tells her story from heaven, where she exists after having been raped, murdered, and dismembered in a frozen cornfield by her neighbor, Mr. Harvey. She introduces her family—her father, Jack; mother, Abigail; sister, Lindsey; and brother, Buckley—the boy she likes, Ray Singh; the lead detective on her case, Len Fenerman; and her heavenly intake counselor, Franny. Susie begins to acclimate to her heaven and learns that it reflects her desires and wishes, and that everyone's heaven is slightly different. With Franny's help, she begins to understand what it means to be dead. She still wants to grow up and live, but now, since she cannot experience actual living, she must be content to watch what happens on earth.

Three days after Susie disappears, Detective Fenerman tells Jack the police have found a body part. Susie's parents have difficulty dealing with the horror of their daughter's disappearance—neither wants to believe that Susie is dead. In addition to the body part, the police find various objects belonging to Susie that indicate she was killed in the cornfield: a copy of the novel *To Kill a Mockingbird*, her biology notes, a love letter from Ray Singh, and her winter hat. This last item convinces the Salmons of Susie's death.

Ray Singh becomes the police's first suspect. Susie's family does not believe that Ray killed Susie; nevertheless, the police believe that his absence from school on the day she died, his dark skin, and his rather arrogant attitude make him a viable suspect. Despite his alibi, Ray, already considered an outsider by his classmates because he and his family came from India, becomes more socially isolated at school.

Chapters 3-5

Susie continues watching family and friends, and as they go about the business of living, she narrates both recent and past events. When Susie left earth, her spirit inadvertently brushed against Ruth Connors, a girl from school. This contact initiates a connection between the girls. By following Ruth, Susie remains engaged in the daily routines of adolescence.

Through conversations with Franny, Susie realizes her homesickness for her mother. She recalls the candid picture she once took of her mother that captured Abigail as a woman, rather than as Mrs. Salmon, wife and mother. When the film was developed, she did not share this picture of her mother; instead, she hid it in her room. Susie watches now as Lindsey enters Susie's room and finds that picture of their mother. Like Susie, Lindsey gets a glimpse of Abigail as Abigail.

Up to this point, Susie has only watched the

living, but now she materializes, revealing herself to her father. She sees Jack smash his collection of ships in a bottle that he and Susie built together. As her father stands amid the wreckage, evidence of his rage and grief, Susie reveals herself in the myriad shards.

Susie recounts what happened after Harvey killed her. He dismantles the underground hole in the cornfield, carries Susie's body parts to his house in a cloth sack, and showers to remove her blood from his body. Then he places Susie's dismembered body in an old safe and drops it in a nearby sinkhole. Returning from the sinkhole, he finds Susie's silver charm bracelet in his pocket. He drives to an industrial park under construction, removes one charm—the Pennsylvania keystone from her father—and throws the bracelet into the construction site. Susie discovers she was not his first victim.

Weeks later, Jack stops to watch Harvey build a ceremonial tent in his yard. Jack volunteers to help with the project, and the two men—Susie's murderer and her father—work side by side. Susie tries to send her father a message, but fails. However, Jack does feel Susie's presence and begins to wonder about Harvey. He believes this strange man knows something about Susie's murder.

Each of the Salmons develops ways to cope with his or her individual grief and fear. Jack involves himself in finding Susie's killer; Abigail isolates herself from her family and turns to Detective Fenerman for answers; Buckley asks direct questions regarding Susie's absence; and Lindsey struggles with both her desire to claim an identity separate from Susie, the dead daughter and sister, and her tremendous grief at the loss of that sibling.

Detective Fenerman talks with Harvey after Jack suggests he might be involved. Harvey expresses his sympathies regarding Susie's murder and explains to the detective that Jack helped him build a ceremonial bridal tent in honor of his deceased wife. Although Detective Fenerman considers Harvey odd, he seems satisfied with Harvey's explanations. Jack, however, is not.

On Christmas Day, Samuel Heckler stops by the Salmon house with a gift for Lindsey. While Samuel and Lindsey talk in the kitchen and later exchange their first kiss, Buckley plays Monopoly with his father. During the game, Jack explains to his young son that Susie is never coming home.

Chapters 6-10

Susie recalls the first time she and Ray Singh "almost" kissed. Two weeks before she died, Susie got to school late and Ray, who cut his first period class, was sitting atop a scaffold in the auditorium. Susie joined him, and as they talked, she realized that Ray was going to kiss her. However, voices from below interrupted them. Susie and Ray watched as the principal and the art teacher chastised Ruth for her charcoal drawings of "real women." When the adults left, Susie and Ray climbed down, and Susie asked to see Ruth's sketchbook. Impressed by the drawings, Susie changed her perspective of Ruth, seeing her as special rather than strange. The girls do not become friends, but after her murder, Susie grows to love the girl she touched as she left earth. Ray and Susie kiss a week later by their lockers. After Susie's death, Ruth and Ray develop a deep friendship, bonding over the death of Susie.

In his effort to make sense of Susie's death, Jack seeks out Ray. At the Singhs' house, Jack talks to Ray's mother. When he confesses his suspicions about Harvey, Ruana Singh validates his theory and tells Jack that given the same circumstances, she would kill her child's murderer.

Ruana's understanding contrasts with Abigail's lack of understanding, further highlighting the widening chasm between Susie's parents. While Jack is at the Singhs' house, Detective Fenerman drops by the Salmons' home. Susie watches as a subtle but discernable attraction develops between her mother and the detective.

Susie's maternal grandmother, Grandma Lynn, arrives to attend Susie's memorial. Lynn, an eccentric and flamboyant personality, brings some vitality into the Salmon home. She begins a lively banter with Jack, gives beauty lessons to Lindsey, and prods Abigail into laughter. She realizes, regardless of the family's tragedy, Lindsey is moving into womanhood and helps her granddaughter by acknowledging this fact. She aids in putting together an outfit for Lindsey to wear to the memorial. Grandma Lynn also answers Lindsey's questions regarding Jack's suspicions about Harvey, who, along with the family, school friends, teachers, neighbors, and Detective Fenerman, attends the memorial. Grandma Lynn does something that Susie notes as important: she identifies Harvey for Lindsey.

Lindsey spends a month of the summer at a statewide gifted symposium. Samuel and Ruth also attend the camp. While they do not become friends, Ruth and Lindsey do share a conversation about Susie. Ruth tells Lindsey she dreams about Susie, and Lindsey admits how much she misses her sister. She also confesses she loves Samuel. As Lindsey and Samuel move toward sexual intimacy, Susie learns sex can be loving rather than violent.

Chapters 11-12

Susie knows Harvey is a serial killer of little girls and, from her heaven, scrutinizes the interior of Harvey's house, which has an identical floor plan to that of the Salmons. But while Susie's house contains markers of family life, Harvey's holds the trophies of his killings as well as the presence of his victims.

Jack becomes more obsessed with finding Susie's killer. Detective Fenerman tells Jack he must stop phoning the police about Harvey. According to the detective, no evidence exists connecting Harvey to Susie's murder. Jack, however, refuses to accept the detective's explanation, as does Lindsey, who overhears the conversation between her father and the detective.

One night, Jack sees a light moving toward the cornfield. Convinced the light belongs to Harvey, Jack grabs a baseball bat and heads for the cornfield intent on vengeance. In fact, the light belongs to Clarissa, Susie's best friend, as she heads to meet her boyfriend Brian. As Jack hollers at whom he believes is Harvey, he hears Clarissa whimpering. Thinking another young girl is in danger, Jack loses all sense of reality. Jack's rage and Clarissa's screams spur Brian, who arrives in the cornfield in time to witness what he believes is Jack's attack on Clarissa, to beat Susie's father with the baseball bat. The beating sends Jack to the hospital for surgery on his damaged knee.

Lindsey arrives at the hospital soon after the incident, expecting to see both her father and mother, but she finds her father alone in his room. Abigail, unable to cope with her collapsing world, seeks out Fenerman. When the detective arrives, he and Abigail go outside onto a small service balcony where physical intimacy enters their relationship.

Chapters 13-16

As the first anniversary of Susie's death approaches, the effects of her death on the living become more apparent, as do the changes involved with growing up. Lindsey becomes not only the sister of the murdered girl but also the daughter of a crazy man. Buckley enters kindergarten and receives special attention because of his sister's murder and grows closer to his father. He also looks to Lindsey for his needs rather than to his mother. Abigail and Jack become further estranged, unable to find comfort in each other. Whereas Jack turns to his living children, Lindsey and Buckley, to help assuage his grief, Abigail finds solace in her relationship with Len and in private reverie.

Although he no longer talks about his certainty that Harvey killed Susie, Jack has not given up that belief, a fact he shares with Lindsey. Lindsey wonders why Fenerman has not arrested him. Jack explains that the police have found no real evidence linking their neighbor to the murder. Lindsey understands the importance of finding something tangible of Susie's in Harvey's house.

Grandma Lynn arrives for Thanksgiving. She quickly picks up on Abigail's affair with Fenerman and also understands that Abigail wants to leave her family. Abigail and Lynn go for a walk and share a rare mother-daughter conversation. Lynn seems to understand more clearly Abigail's desires and disappointments.

Lindsey decides to search Harvey's house. She watches and plans, and when she sees him leave, she breaks a basement window, enters the house, and begins the search. As Susie watches Lindsey in the house, she sees what Lindsey sees and also sees Harvey's previous victims. While Susie finds supernatural evidence of Harvey's crimes, Lindsey finds tangible evidence linking him to Susie's murder—drawings of the hole in the cornfield with

"Stolfuz cornfield" written on one of them. Harvey arrives home while Lindsey continues her search. Despite her caution, he hears her in the upstairs bedroom. Lindsey escapes through the window, but he glimpses her leaving his yard—catching the number on her soccer jersey—and he knows it is Lindsey.

When Lindsey returns home, she finds her parents and Samuel frantic over her late arrival. She tells her father about breaking into Harvey's house and shows him what she found. In heaven, Susie meets the other girls Harvey has murdered.

Before calling the police, Harvey hides the knife he used to kill Susie and the charms he took from his other victims. As the police talk with Harvey about the breakin, Jack phones Fenerman, but he is not there. At Harvey's house, the officers seem satisfied with his account of events. Harvey does not, however, mention the stolen drawings. When the officers bring them to his attention, Harvey offers the explanation that he was trying to figure out how Susie's murder occurred.

While Jack tries to reach Fenerman and the police talk with Mr. Harvey, Abigail meets Fenerman for a rendezvous, thus the detective misses the call that would have put him on Harvey's trail. Shaken by the breakin and understanding the implications of the drawings Lindsey took of the hole in the cornfield, Harvey packs up and leaves the area.

By the one-year anniversary of Susie's death,

Ray and Ruth's friendship deepens, moving beyond a platonic attachment to one that includes some degree of physical intimacy. The two friends decide to commemorate Susie's death with a visit to the cornfield. When they arrive, they find Samuel and his brother Hal already there. Shortly, neighbors gather at the site of Susie's murder. Some bring candles, lighting up the evening with an impromptu memorial. When Lindsey notices the lights in the cornfield, she urges her mother to attend. Abigail declines, and in the ensuing conversation with her mother, Lindsey realizes her mother plans to leave the family. Lindsey, Buckley, and Jack join their friends and neighbors in the cornfield.

"Snapshots"

As time progresses, Susie watches the lives of those on earth unfold: Abigail leaves Pennsylvania, ultimately for California; Grandma Lynn comes to stay; Lindsey learns of Abigail and Fenerman's relationship; Buckley must now deal with the loss of his mother. Samuel's brother, Hal, using his biker connections, gets a lead on Harvey, which he passes on to Fenerman. The police are finally able to prove Harvey's guilt, but he has vanished and Fenerman feels tremendous guilt for not having listened to Jack. Ray goes to Penn State University to study medicine, and Ruth moves to New York, taking up a bohemian life, certain that she possess a psychic connection with murdered women and children.

Chapters 17-20

Lindsey and Samuel graduate from Temple University in Philadelphia. Caught in a rainstorm on their motorcycle ride home from the ceremony, they find an abandoned house, where Samuel proposes to Lindsey.

Buckley, now in seventh grade, uses old clothes he found in the basement to tie his tomato plants to their stakes. As Jack watches, he recognizes the clothes as Susie's and forbids his son to use them. Buckley lashes out at his father, accusing him of putting the dead Susie before both his living children. As father and son argue, Jack suffers a heart attack.

Jack hovers between life and death, with Susie wishing him to join her in her heaven and Buckley holding him to earth. As Susie turns from the events on earth, she meets her paternal grandfather in her heaven; they dance together.

Abigail flies home to be with Jack in the hospital. Lindsey, Samuel, and Buckley meet her at the airport. Having not seen her children for almost a decade, Abigail is apprehensive. The reunion is strained, with Lindsey cautious and Buckley angry. Her reunion with Jack proves as tenuous as the first meeting with her children.

Abigail struggles with the decision to return to California or to stay with her family. Her introspection reveals that she left because of her inability to cope with the guilt generated by Susie's death. She realizes she does indeed love Jack and her children and decides to stay. Jack begins to understand he must accept Abigail for who she is. Finally able to talk about Susie, Jack and Abigail cry together.

Chapters 21-23

Ray and Ruth both return home and go to the sinkhole, which is scheduled to be filled and paved over. Harvey also makes his way back to his old neighborhood, hoping to kill Lindsey. He, too, heads for the sinkhole. While at the sinkhole, Susie's presence overwhelms Ruth, and Susie falls to earth and into Ruth's body. In the meantime, police have recovered Susie's keystone charm at a Connecticut murder site; Fenerman returns the charm to Jack and Abigail.

As Susie inhabits Ruth's body, Ruth leaves the earth. Ray senses a change in Ruth and comes to believe that somehow Ruth has become Susie or vice versa. Susie, using Ruth's body, finally experiences the culmination of a developing sexuality as she and Ray make love. Although Susie must once again leave the earth, this time her leave-taking proves gentle and gradual instead of violent and abrupt. Ray and Ruth try to make sense of the events that occur.

Susie finally lets go of her family, even though she will always watch over them. Jack leaves the hospital. Individually, the Salmons have each confronted his or her grief, guilt, anger, and fear, thus making it possible for them to reconstruct the family unit. Together and separately, they move beyond Susie's death.

"Bones"

The lives of the dead integrate into the lives of the living. Susie's family members cannot and do not forget her, nor do they allow their memories of her to keep them from moving on. Harvey finally gets justice when he is hit by a falling icicle and falls unconscious into a ravine, where falling snow covers his body.

Clarissa

Clarissa is Susie's best friend. Her clandestine meeting in the cornfield with her boyfriend, Brian, leads to Brian's attack on Jack.

Media Adaptations

- Recorded Books published an unabridged edition of *The Lovely Bones* on audio CD in August 2002.

Ruth Connors

Ruth, the girl Susie inadvertently brushes

against as the she departs earth, is artistic and poetic with a feminist sensibility, existing on the fringes of junior high and high school society. She moves to New York after graduation, living a bohemian life of writing poetry, communing with Susie, and recording in her journal the deaths of women and children, deaths that she sees in dreams and visions. Because of her psychic connection to the spirit of murdered women and children, Ruth provides the means for Susie to revisit earth and consummate her relationship with Ray. Ruth also develops and maintains a strong friendship with Ray.

Detective Len Fenerman

Len Fenerman is the lead detective on Susie's murder case. A small but tenacious man, Fenerman believes that he will find Susie's killer. He understands the horror of unexplained death, as his wife committed suicide. Fenerman carries Susie's picture, as well as the pictures of victims of unsolved murder cases, in his wallet. Although he knows that he should not give in to his feelings for Abigail, he eventually begins an affair with her. Because of his cautiousness regarding Harvey, Susie's killer, Fenerman fails to arrest him. This failure haunts the detective, and he must bear the guilt of his decisions.

Franny

Franny, a social worker on earth, is Susie's intake counselor in heaven. She also serves as a surrogate mother.

George Harvey

George Harvey, a thirty-six-year-old single man, is a serial killer who rapes and murders Susie. Although considered odd by his neighbors, Harvey does not draw attention to himself. He builds dollhouses and possesses a fascination with buildings. Taught to steal by his mother and then abandoned by her, and raised by a tyrannical father, Harvey lacks both a conscience and social skills. He fits the profile of a sociopath, reliving the murders in his mind, deriving intense pleasure from the killings, and taking trophies from his victims. When Lindsey breaks into his house and takes evidence linking him to Susie's murder, Mr. Harvey's ordered world begins to disintegrate. He leaves town, eventually coming back determined to kill Lindsey, but a combination of circumstances prevent him from doing so.

Hal Heckler

Hal is Samuel's older brother. He rides and repairs motorcycles. After Harvey's disappearance, Hal uses his network of biker friends to search for him. Hal eventually passes on some key information to Detective Fenerman.

Samuel Heckler

Samuel is Lindsey's childhood sweetheart and

eventually marries her. Samuel helps Lindsey cope with her sister's death, her mother's abandonment, and her father's heart attack. Samuel, along with his brother, Hal, becomes an integral part of the Salmon family. He and Hal treat Buckley, Lindsey's little brother, like their own brother. Samuel loves carpentry and restoring old houses, a passion that he turns into a career. This passion for fixing broken and battered things parallels his ability to alleviate Lindsey's pain, name Jack's overprotectiveness, and deflect Buckley's anger.

Holly

Holly is Susie's roommate in heaven. Although she and Susie share much of their heaven, Holly also has a heaven to which Susie has no access. Holly helps Susie understand heaven.

Grandma Lynn

Grandma Lynn, Susie's grandmother and Abigail's mother, is eccentric, colorful and drinks too much. Prior to Susie's murder, her visits to the Salmon's upended routines and delighted her grandchildren. Not overly motherly, Lynn has a strained relationship with her daughter. When Abigail leaves, Lynn provides the stability that keeps the family together. She helps Lindsey grow into womanhood, and she helps Buckley negotiate his anger and hurt.

Brian Nelson

Brian is Clarissa's boyfriend. He beats Mr. Salmon with a baseball bat when he mistakenly thinks that Susie's father is attacking Clarissa in the cornfield.

Abigail Salmon

Abigail is Susie's mother. She is college educated, with a master's degree in literature and aspirations to teach. In the early years of her marriage to Jack, Abigail possessed a passionate nature but found that the demands of motherhood pulled her away from her husband and from her own dreams. As her family grew, Abigail became less involved with her children and husband. Nevertheless, Susie's death unsettles her, and she finds no outlet for her grief. She embarks on an affair with Detective Fenerman but does not love him. Her need to find herself, reclaim her place in the world as an individual, and escape her intense grief propel her to relocate to California. There she seems to find some solace, working in a vineyard and leaving motherhood and wifehood behind. However, she comes to realize that she can leave neither of those things, and when she returns to Pennsylvania, she also realizes that she viewed Susie's death as punishment for own failings as a mother. This understanding allows her to rebuild her relationship with her husband and with her children. These things do not prove easy, but Abigail does reclaim her position within the family, albeit a changed family—reconfigured by Susie's absence as well as by Abigail's.

Buckley Salmon

Buckley is the youngest of the three Salmon children. He is four years old at the time of Susie's murder and seven years old when his mother leaves. These two events force Buckley to develop emotional defenses in order to survive the pain of abandonment. He believes that he has supernatural encounters with Susie. Both Grandma Lynn and Lindsey act as maternal surrogates, and Buckley develops a close relationship with his father. As he matures, he becomes protective of his father and of Lindsey. When Abigail returns, Buckley is hateful, sullen, and very angry.

Jack Salmon

Jack is Susie's father. In the aftermath of her murder, Jack deals not only with his own grief and anger but also seeks to assuage Lindsey's emotions and protect Buckley from the hurt. Like Abigail, Jack must also work through some guilt generated by his daughter's death. He questions his position as father and protector when he realizes that he was not there to save his little girl. His frustration at this failure fuels his need to be active in the police investigation. Jack cannot remain passive as the police fail to develop leads. He never wavers in his conviction that Mr. Harvey murdered Susie, and once the police disregard his theories, Jack turns to

Lindsey, sharing his thoughts with her. Despite his closeness to Lindsey and Buckley, Jack retains a strong connection to Susie, feeling her presence, talking to her, refusing to let her place in his family's life fade. Whereas Abigail withdraws into almost a state of indifference, Jack builds ties that may bind too tightly. Finally, Jack understands that in order to have a strong family, he must loosen the bonds, and he does what the living must do in order to go on living—let go of the dead. In addition, Jack does what parents must do: let go of their children. Jack can make these moves only after he turns inward and faces his own fears and weaknesses.

Lindsey Salmon

Lindsey is the middle child of the three Salmon children. Bright, articulate, athletic, blonde, and pretty, Lindsey, one year younger than Susie, is amazingly close to her sister, so Susie's death leaves a deep void in Lindsey's life. However, she refuses to be the dead girl's sister, the living daughter, the reminder of the missing girl. Lindsey struggles through the ordinary traumas of adolescence, but Susie's murder, Abigail's distance, Jack's need to find the killer, and Buckley's dependence all complicate the process for her. With Grandma Lynn's help, Samuel's devotion, and her own determination, Lindsey develops into a strong young woman, and she risks her own safety in order to find proof of Harvey's guilt. Lindsey does not, however, betray her dreams. Unlike her mother, she follows her aspirations. She graduates from college, gets an advanced degree, and takes up a career. Although Lindsey never leaves Susie behind, she does move beyond Susie's death.

Susie Salmon

Susie, the narrator, is a fourteen-year-old girl and the eldest of the three Salmon children. She is raped and murdered by her neighbor, Mr. Harvey, as she walks home from junior high. Susie is spunky and curious, a dreamer with a desire to be a wildlife photographer, and looks forward to high school and to growing up. Susie shares a special relationship with her father—helping him to build ships in a bottle. She and sister Lindsey are close, and she plays mother hen to little brother Buckley. Susie adores her mother and seems to understand her mother's need for privacy.

Seldom is Susie a direct participant in the action; usually, she observes and reflects. Sometimes, however, she makes her presence known to the living—in the shards of glass from her father's broken ships in a bottle, in a dim appearance at a family gathering, in the body of Ruth Connors. She is with Lindsey as she searches Mr. Harvey's house, leading her sister into the upstairs rooms. In addition, much of the action takes place because of someone's longing for, search for, or love for Susie. So, indirectly, Susie influences individual decisions and outcomes.

Just as Lindsey must figure out how to grow up—what it means to live, Susie must figure out what it means not to grow up—what it means to be dead. She learns that like the living, she, too, must journey. Susie also learns that the dead, like the living, must let go, not easy for a girl who wants so desperately to live.

Susie does return to earth. She falls into Ruth's body, initiated partly by Susie's longing to kiss Ray one more time and see where that kiss would lead, and also by Ruth's desire to understand the dead, to see them. Ruth desires to leave earth, and Susie desires to return. After this incident, Susie watches with love and pleasure as her family reconfigures into a new family, one that does and does not include her.

Ray Singh

Ray is the boy with whom Susie shares her first kiss. Born in India and raised in England until his family moved to the United States, Ray is dark skinned and well-spoken. He writes Susie a love letter that she never gets to read. This letter, which the police find in the cornfield, initially leads them to suspect Ray of the murder. Like Ruth, Ray inhabits the periphery of junior high society. He finds himself drawn to Ruth's quirkiness, her love of art and literature, and her connection to Susie. Together, Ray and Ruth speculate about Susie's murder. Ray maintains a close relationship with Ruth throughout high school as well as after graduation, when he goes to Penn State and Ruth to New York. Susie longs for Ray as she watches him from heaven. When she returns to earth in Ruth's body, Ray recognizes the change in Ruth, calling her Susie. He makes love to her, and he asks her to tell him about heaven. This encounter affects Ray when he begins to practice medicine; he refuses to consider only medical or scientific explanations regarding death.

Ruana Singh

Ruana is Ray's mother. She is an exotic personality, dignified and calm when the police question her son about Susie's murder. Ruana possesses deep empathy for the Salmons, and she plays an important role in Jack's determination to avenge Susie's death. Ruana listens to his theories regarding Mr. Harvey and legitimizes Jack's desire for revenge. Before Abigail leaves, the two women share a moment together, and Ruana understands Abigail's feeling of isolation. After Abigail leaves, Ruana often bakes apple pies for the Salmons, which she has Ray deliver.

Loss and Grief

Loss of a loved one and the stages of mourning or grief manifest as overriding themes in *The Lovely Bones*. Through the voice of Susie Salmon, the fourteen-year-old narrator of the novel, readers get an in-depth look at the grieving process. Susie focuses more on the aftermath and effects of her murder and rape on her family rather than on the event itself. She watches her parents and sister move through the five stages of grief: denial, anger, bargaining, depression, and acceptance. However, Alice Sebold makes clear that these categories do not necessarily remain rigid and that individuals deal with grief in various ways. For example, Abigail, Susie's mother, withdraws from her living children, Lindsey and Buckley, whereas Jack, her husband, draws closer to them. Lindsey, Susie's sister, vacillates between denial and acceptance, sometimes exhibiting both elements simultaneously. In addition, Sebold expands the definitions of both loss and grief by including Susie herself in the process. If readers limit their understanding of grief to losing and coping with the death of a loved one, then they have trouble accounting for Susie's emotions. She mourns her own death and the missed opportunity of getting to grow up, but more significantly, Susie grieves over the loss of living people. In other words, the novel extends the grieving process to include the dead themselves.

By including Susie in this process and having Abigail leave the family, Sebold investigates the nature of loss and its relationship to grief. The novel suggests change equals loss, which in turn initiates grief. While Susie's death emerges as the most blatant change in the lives of the Salmons, other significant changes also occur. Lindsey changes from adolescent to adult; Buckley changes from child to adolescent; Jack changes from a man secure in his place in the family to one questioning his ability to hold the family together; and Abigail changes from a woman questioning her position as wife and mother to one who redefines and then embraces that position. While each of these changes generates a sense of loss, ultimately each character moves on from the loss and grief. In *The Lovely Bones*, both the living and dead learn letting go opens up possibilities.

Life and Death

On some level, all literature investigates the nature of human experience or the human condition. Certainly life and death constitute the two most significant experiences of being human, and as such, much literature deals with these two issues. *The Lovely Bones* pointedly asks two questions: "What does it mean to be alive?" and "What does it mean to be dead?"

As Susie learns what being dead means, she must deal with what being alive means as well. The fact she can no longer experience the physical world —that she can no longer experience living— emerges as her biggest disappointment. The novel then offers experiencing the physical as an attribute of living. Although denied this aspect of living, the dead Susie can engage in the human condition of wanting, wishing, and desiring. Thus Sebold blurs the lines between what constitutes life and death. Susie clearly understands she is dead. She knows she inhabits a realm different from earth, but in many ways, not completely separate from it. After all, Susie's heaven looks earthly, not celestial, and she participates in activities that associate much more closely with earth than heaven: eating ice cream, romping with dogs, living in a duplex.

The novel presents life as a series of changes, all of which involve the body and the physical environment—physicality seems the defining characteristic of life. The event that allows Susie to move on in her heaven, or to move on in death, is her return to earth. Although she has "returned" in a disembodied form, when she inhabits Ruth's body, Susie "realize[s] that the marvelous weight weighing [her] down was the weight of the human body." Yet Susie understands the temporariness of this corporality, but perhaps that realization is precisely one of Sebold's points.

Coming of Age and Rites of Passage

The coming-of-age novel involves the

initiation of the protagonist into adulthood. This initiation usually occurs through the acquisition of knowledge and experience. In many of these novels, the move into adulthood includes a loss of innocence or the destruction of a false sense of security. The protagonist often experiences a shift from ignorance to knowledge, innocence to experience, idealism to realism, or immaturity to maturity. In addition, coming of age involves rituals or rites of passage. *The Lovely Bones* focuses on these issues as the author explores the process of growing up.

The novel begins when Lindsey Salmon is thirteen years old and ends almost ten years later, with Lindsey as wife and mother. It traces her move through the routines and events of female adolescence—first kisses, shaving of legs, makeup, summer camp, love, friendship, college. The novel, however, also traces Susie's coming of age. By presenting the development of a dead girl along with a living one, Sebold imbues the experiences of growing up with enhanced significance. Susie cannot move on in death until she finishes "growing up."

Susie's rape and murder hastens the process of moving from innocence to experience for both girls. Susie learns her suburban and rather ordinary world is not safe—men murder children in this world. She moves swiftly and violently from innocence to experience, and from idealism to realism. Yet this shift does not culminate in her "coming of age;" rather, it initiates a need for her to experience these things more slowly and more naturally. While Susie's death also hastens Lindsey's loss of innocence, it does so less dramatically. Although Lindsey understands that her world is not particularly safe, that bad people exist and that these people do bad things, she still participates in the normal rituals of growing up.

Like many teenage girls, Lindsey experiments with makeup and with finding a style that suits her. She experiences a tender first kiss with Samuel, and they move slowly through the rituals of courtship. She grows into her sexuality, developing a relationship based on trust, gentleness, and understanding. However, Susie's murder, combined with her mother's absence, pushes Lindsey into adult roles early in her life. So while acknowledging the naturalness of growing up, Sebold also contextualizes that experience. In *The Lovely Bones*, moving from a place of innocence to one of knowledge can occur violently and abruptly. Coming of age can happen in circumstances that circumvent the normal, perhaps suggesting a need to rethink normal.

Style

Point of View

In *The Lovely Bones*, point of view, the perspective from which the story is told, plays a crucial role in the narrative. Generally, a novel's point of view consists of one of four traditional stances: first person, second person, third person, and third person omniscient. First person point of view presents the events of the story from the perception of a single character. Second person point of view involves the author telling the story as if it is happening to the reader. With third person point of view, the reader has no insight into the character's minds; therefore, he or she must make sense of the action as it takes place. Third person omniscient offers a "godlike" perspective, transcending time or place, allowing the reader to see the actions and to look into the minds of the characters to know their thoughts, feelings and motives.

Alice Sebold presents a story told from an omniscient first person point of view, the perspective of Susie Salmon, who is dead. Susie, from her vantage point in heaven, sees everything—actions, motivations, thoughts—so her narration functions like third person omniscient, except that she tells the story in first person. Susie's access to the minds of other characters provides readers with this same access. In addition, as an omniscient first person narrator telling the story from beyond the limitations of earthly time, she also can and does experience many of the characters' memories. For example, she sees and relates incidents from her killer, Mr. Harvey's, childhood and his past killings. Because of her omniscience, Susie often glimpses intensely personal thoughts and actions, such as her mother's first tryst with Detective Fenerman, or her mother's internal thoughts about motherhood.

Topics for Further Study

- Elisabeth Kübler-Ross, M.D., developed the five-stage grief model, which outlines and defines the stages that a grieving person goes through while healing. Research this model, list and define the five terms, then write an essay explaining how Jack Salmon,

Abigail Salmon, and Susie Salmon in Alice Sebold's *The Lovely Bones* progress through each stage.

- What would have happened if Susie were never killed by Mr. Harvey? Knowing what you do about her desires, interests, and goals, do you think Susie's life would have turned out more like Abigail's or Lindsey's? Would Susie have married Ray, or lived a bohemian life in the city like Ruth? Write a short biography of Susie's life, including her family, that addresses who Susie might have been if she had not been murdered at age fourteen.

- Using some historical research on the Women's Movement in the 1970s, explain how Abigail Salmon, Lindsey Salmon, Ruth Connors, and Ruana Singh in Sebold's *The Lovely Bones* exemplify elements of that movement. In other words, what aspect of the Women's Movement does each of these women illustrate? Write an essay incorporating your research into your explanation.

- One can easily read Sebold's *The Lovely Bones* as a coming-of-age story. Identify which characters "come of age" and why. What does the novel offer as the rites of passage for growing up? Do these rites seem bound by the time frame of the novel? In an essay, compare the rites and rituals of adolescence presented in *The Lovely Bones* with those of today's teenagers. Try to account for any differences by addressing relevant cultural, political, or social issues.

This combination of third person omniscient and first person points of view proves an innovative move on Sebold's part. Few novels offer the perspective of a dead protagonist—especially one who has been brutally raped and murdered. However, this new point of view makes the disturbing subject matter bearable and also allows Sebold to inject some humor and lightness into a rather horrifying story. Because she sees everything and because she relates what she sees, Susie provides the reader with opportunities to sympathize and or identify with various characters. In addition, because this omniscient viewpoint filters through a first person or personal voice, it also emerges as a specific perspective: sometimes angry, sometimes confused, sometimes spunky, and sometimes humorous, which carries with it a distinctive personality.

Setting

Setting includes the time, place, and culture in

which the action of the narrative takes place. Time and place emerge as crucial elements in understanding the setting in *The Lovely Bones*. Traditionally, time can involve three elements: historical period, duration, and the perception of time by the characters. Sebold uses dates at various points throughout the narrative; in fact, the novel opens with a specific date, December 6, 1973. Immediately, the reader understands the historical time—the early 1970s—as well as the seasonal time —winter. However, as the story progresses, the historical periods shift as Susie takes the reader into the past and alludes to the future. For example, after giving us the date of her death, she offers a contemporary reference to the pictures of missing children on milk cartons and in the daily mail. This reference raises questions regarding the time period from which Susie is telling the story. Sebold's use of time shifts—the narration slides among past, present, and future—ties very closely to elements of place.

Like the shifts in time, the location of the story shifts between heaven and earth. Most of the action itself occurs on earth with the telling occurring in heaven. Some action does, however, take place in heaven: Susie meets Mr. Harvey's other victims in heaven; she and her roommate, Holly, explore; she dances with her grandfather. However, these actions do not necessarily propel the plot (the pattern of carefully selected events), but they do expand the story (all the events which are to be depicted). Both place and time closely relate to the coming-of-age element in the book, as well as to the themes of loss and grief.

Foreshadowing and Flashback

For the most part, Sebold's novel follows the traditional structure of plot. However, the events do not necessarily unfold in chronological fashion. For instance, the novel opens with Susie's murder, and as events unfold, establishes a relationship between events. To understand the causality, the reader needs background information, which Sebold presents through the use of flashback, a device that offers actions that occurred before the beginning of the story. Once Sebold establishes the murder, she has Susie look backward to how the murder occurred. As with point of view and setting, Sebold also complicates the traditional idea of plot. For example, in chapter one, Susie discusses her murder and includes a detail about a neighborhood dog finding her elbow and bringing it home. However, the actual incident of the dog finding the elbow and the police telling her parents about it occurs weeks after the murder. These occurrences in the story are moments of foreshadowing, which create expectation. Through the use of flashback and foreshadowing, Sebold veers away from a strictly chronological unfolding of events; rather, plot becomes more circular even while the narrative progressive chronologically through the 1970s.

Historical Context

Alice Sebold wrote *The Lovely Bones* in the late 1990s; the book first appeared in print in June 2002; and the story takes place in the 1970s. All of these dates prove significant. At the time of the writing, America was facing both a new decade and a new millennium. By the late 1990s, Americans saw the creation of the World Wide Web; engaged in debates over health care, social security reform, gun control; watched national sex scandals unfold (the Tailhook affair and the Bill Clinton/Monica Lewinski affair); sat riveted to the O. J. Simpson murder trial; and were stunned by the violence of the 1999 shooting at Columbine High School in Colorado. Sebold penned her story amid a growing awareness of, and concern with, issues of domestic, sexual, and teen violence. In many ways, her novel reflects these concerns as it reflects the cultural climate of the 1990s.

Its publication date, however, carries added significance. The novel, released less than a year after the September 11, 2001, attacks on the World Trade Center in New York and the Pentagon in Washington D.C., speaks directly to a nation's need for comfort. *The Lovely Bones* made its debut in an America forever stripped of its belief that terrorism and random violence happens elsewhere. The social and cultural atmosphere at this time radiated fear, distrust, sadness, anger, and grief. Although Sebold wrote this novel before the attacks, the subject matter echoes the contemporaneous concerns of America.

The novel also draws on the historical, cultural, social, and political issues of the 1970s. In many ways, America "came of age" in the 1970s as social change, discontent with the government, advances in civil rights for minorities and women, environmental concerns, and space exploration defined the decade. The Vietnam War, which sparked antiwar protests and student demonstrations, and the Watergate Scandal, which resulted in the resignation of a president, shattered the last vestiges of a naive America. Other changes arose in the 1970s that added to America's cultural and social climate, including the women's movement. Women's places in American life expanded into political and professional areas, and people began to question the traditional gender roles of women and men.

The changes of the 1970s figure into *The Lovely Bones* in several ways: first, through Sebold's female characters. Ruth Connors embodies the feminism of the 1970s with her avant-garde approach to her drawings, poetry, and reading. She refuses the constraints of the status quo in these areas as well as in the arena of acceptably feminine behavior and attire. However, whereas Ruth overtly embraces feminism, Susie's mother, Abigail, struggles to name her discontent. Abigail illustrates many of the women in the 1970s who did not publicly espouse feminism, yet whose desire to transcend the constraints of motherhood and wifehood drew on feminist principles. Secondly, the novel reflects the 1970s concern with the environment through the encroachment of building and industry into the Salmons' suburban neighborhood. Finally, the disturbing subject matter of a child's rape and murder, and Susie's refusal to sanitize the images of her death reflect the horrific pictures of the dead and dismembered of the Vietnam War. During the 1970s, images of violence entered the homes of suburban Americans through the television, and for the first time, Americans watched a war—complete with all of its horrors—from their living rooms. In *The Lovely Bones*, the tangible marks of violence that enter suburbia are not media images of war dead; rather, those marks are the objects of a raped and murdered girl.

Critical Overview

The Lovely Bones enjoyed immediate popular success from the time of its publication. The novel, published in June 2002, topped the *New York Times* bestseller list that summer. Prior its publication, as Charlotte Abbot notes in *Publishers Weekly*, bestselling author Anna Quindlen told viewers of the *Today Show*, "If you read one book this summer, it should be *The Lovely Bones* by Alice Sebold. It's destined to be a classic along the lines of *To Kill a Mockingbird*, and it's one of the best books I've read in years." For the most part, the novel garnered excellent reviews after its publications, with critics praising the first person omniscient point of view and the stunning opening pages.

In a review for *Christian Century*, Stephen H. Webb argues that Sebold's reworked point of view "is the only way to fully comprehend such an intolerable tragedy [the rape and murder of a fourteen-year-old girl]." Writing for the *London Review of Books*, Rebecca Mead deems Susie "a bright and ironical observer," and Michiko Kakutani, in her front-page review of *The Lovely Bones* in the *New York Times*, points out that the narrator possesses a "matter-of-fact charm." Finally, in his review in the *Christian Science Monitor*, Ron Charles writes, "The power of *The Lovely Bones* flows from this voice, a voice at once charmingly adolescent and tragically mature." Most reviewers identify Susie's voice as one of the novel's strong points.

Critics also agree on another of the novel's strengths: the opening pages. Even unfavorable reviews praised Sebold's compelling opening. In Daniel Mendelsohn's review in the *New York Review of Books*, he likens the novel to TV movies of the week—artificial, contrived, and lightweight. However, Mendelsohn also writes, "The novel begins strikingly…. The few pages that follow … are the best in the book," and he praises the authenticity of these pages. Writing for the *Guardian*, Ali Smith slams *The Lovely Bones* for its timidity and sentimentality, but finds "the opening chapters … shattering and dazzling in their mix of horror and normality." Despite a handful of negative reviews, the novel has been the "breakout fiction debut of the year" that Lev Grossman predicted in the book section of the July 1, 2002, edition of *Time* magazine.

Sebold's novel does, however, exhibit some weaknesses, and even her most ardent admirers recognize them. Kakutani comments that Sebold stumbles in the "highly abstract musing on Susie belonging to a historical continuum of murdered girls and women," and this critic finds the scenes dealing with Susie's classmate, Ruth Connor's, "belief that she can … channel Susie's feelings" unconvincing. Other critics find troubling Susie's return to earth, which Sarah Churchwell of the *Times Literary Supplement* calls "a false move that violates the contract of willingly suspended disbelief."

Overall, critics believe that the novel's strengths outshine its weak moments. In her *Washington Post* review, Maria Russo considers *The Lovely Bones* "utterly original and deeply affecting," and she asserts that Sebold "manages to put her readers into contact with a throbbing pulse of life." Sebold, says Russo, "has an unusual flair for both owning and transforming dark material." Katherine Bouton of the *New York Times Book Review* concurs. Sebold, she writes, "deals with almost unthinkable subjects with humor and intelligence and a kind of mysterious grace."

What Do I Read Next?

- *Lucky* (1999) is Sebold's memoir of her 1981 rape. In it, she details the rape itself and chronicles the arrest, trial, and conviction of the rapist. She also addresses the emotional aftermath and consequences of the attack.

- Sue Monk Kidd's novel *The Secret Life of Bees* (2003) is a coming-of-age story. Set in the 1960s, *The Secret Life of Bees* deals with tragedy, the absence of a mother, and the protagonist's need to look backward and then to let go in order to move on.

- *The Five People You Meet in Heaven* (2003), by Mitch Albom, follows the protagonist, Eddie, through his last moments on earth, his funeral, and the days after his death. Then the story shifts to Eddie's arrival at and experiences in heaven.

- Aimee Bender's first novel, *An Invisible Sign of My Own* (2000), is about a girl named Mona who deals with her father's mysterious illness by withdrawing from the things she likes to do: eating dessert, playing piano, spending time with her boyfriend. She grows up to become a second-grade math teacher, and must use her own experiences with illness to help a student through her mother's cancer.

- *Family* (1991), by J. California Cooper, is narrated by a dead main character. Clora, a pre-Civil War slave, escapes slavery through suicide. After her death, her spirit narrates the story of her children and grandchildren as they live through slavery and the Civil War.

- *The Afterlife* (2003), by Gary Soto, is the story of Chuy, a murdered seventeen-year-old boy. Now deceased, Chuy must solve the mystery of his murder and come to terms with his new identity in death.

Sources

Abbott, Charlotte, "How About Them Bones?" in *Publishers Weekly*, Vol. 249, No. 30, July 29, 2002, pp. 22-23.

Bouton, Katherine, "What Remains," Review of *The Lovely Bones*, in the *New York Times*, July 14, 2002, Final edition, Section 7, Column 3, p. 14.

Charles, Ron, "'If I Die Before I Wake, I Pray the Lord My Soul to Take': In Alice Sebold's Debut Novel, the Dead Must Learn to Let Go, Too," Review of *The Lovely Bones*, in the *Christian Science Monitor*, July 25, 2002, p. 15.

Churchwell, Sarah, "A Neato Heaven," Review of *The Lovely Bones*, in the *Times Literary Supplement*, No. 5186, August 23, 2002, p. 19.

Friedan, Betty, *The Feminine Mystique*, W.W. Norton, 1997, p. 9.

Grossman, Lev, "Murdered, She Wrote," Review of *The Lovely Bones*,in *Time*, Vol. 160, No. 4, July 1, 2002, p. 62.

Kakutani, Michiko, "The Power of Love Leaps the Great Divide of Death," Review of *The Lovely Bones*, in the *New York Times*, June 18, 2002, Section E, Column 4, p. 1.

Mead, Rebecca, "Immortally Cute," Review of *The Lovely Bones*, in the *London Review of Books*, Vol. 24, No. 20, October 17, 2002, p. 18.

Mendelsohn, Daniel, "Novel of the Year," Review of *The Lovely Bones*, in the *New York Review of Books*, Vol. 50, No. 1, January 16, 2003, pp. 4-5.

Russo, Maria, "Girl, Interrupted," Review of *The Lovely Bones*, in the *Washington Post*, August 11, 2002, p. BWO7.

Sebold, Alice, *The Lovely Bones*, Little Brown, 2004.

——————, "The Oddity of Suburbia," in *The Lovely Bones*, Little Brown, 2004, pp. 2-3.

Smith, Ali, "A Perfect Afterlife," Review of *The Lovely Bones*, in the *Guardian*, August 17, 2002, *Guardian Unlimited*, www.books.guardian.co.uk. (August 17, 2002).

Webb, Stephen H., Earth from Above,? in *Christian Century*, Vol. 119, No. 21, October 9-22, 2002, p. 20.

Woloch, Nancy, *Women and the American Experience*, 3d ed., McGraw-Hill, pp. 508-09.

Further Reading

Baily, Beth L., and David Farber, eds., *America in the Seventies*, University Press of Kansas, 2004.

> America in the Seventies is a collection of essays by leading scholars in the field. These essays address such issues as the cultural despair of the decade; analyze elements of seventies' culture such as film, music, and advertising; and discuss the attempt by Americans to redefine themselves in the 1970s.

Douglas, Susan, *Where the Girls Are: Growing Up Female with the Mass Media*, Three Rivers Press, 1995.

> This book focuses on media images of women in the last fifty years of the twentieth century. Douglas's discussions regarding the 1970s help in contextualizing the cultural atmosphere of Sebold's The Lovely Bones.

Evans, Sarah, *Born for Liberty*, Simon & Schuster, 1997.

> This one-volume history of American women examines the changing role of women in this country. The later chapters,

particularly chapters 11-12, prove helpful in understanding Abigail Salmon and Ruth Connors in Sebold's novel.

Friedan, Betty, *The Feminine Mystique*, Norton, 1963.

The Feminine Mystique, a foundational feminist text, examines the discontent of white, educated, suburban wives and mothers. Although published in the early 1960s, Friedan's study seems relevant to Abigail Salmon's conflicting feelings in The Lovely Bones.

Kübler-Ross, Elisabeth, *On Death and Dying*, Scribner, 1969, reprint, 1997.

This book, written in plain, understandable language, introduces and explains the five stages of grief. It remains a classic in understanding both the dying and grieving processes.

Lightning Source UK Ltd.
Milton Keynes UK
UKHW020642170822
407432UK00010B/1485

9 781375 400473